# Unshakable Peace in an Unsteady World

MILK
&
HONEY
Books

## Name

## Start Date

# Contents

# Introduction

This "Peace" devotional was birthed by a group of women who became unlikely friends. The truth is we, the authors of this book, have never met in-person as of this publication. We fell into the forced rhythms of virtual life thanks to the global pandemic. However, our commitment to be part of a digital group led to something unexpected and beautiful.

Elise, Jodi, Michele, and Jess met in the online community, "Called Creatives." We were in various stages of our careers as writers, podcasters, and marketers. After the first meeting, it was evident our group was divinely appointed. Not in the sense that we immediately knew we were going to create a collaborative project, but because we all became intimately connected. Over the next year, the four of us shared writing projects, life milestones, trials, traumas, and losses. We laughed together, cheered for one another, and cried together. Each of us was transformed by the love, support, and prayers found in this unique community.

We commiserated on the state of our world and local communities. After we had been consistently meeting for about four months, Jodi recommended we do "something" together. Something that would help people get through these very dark days. We all agreed we needed more peace. Unshakable peace.

That "something" became this devotional. Each of us brings a unique perspective, life stage, and personal experience. All of us are mothers and wives, passionate about our faith. Our intention with writing this devotional was to equip the reader with the tools, encouragement, and insight to discover peace in an unsteady world.

You will read stories about overcoming anxiety, fighting for rest, and seeking silver linings. Each devotional is anchored in Scripture, personalized with reflection questions, and bookended by prayer.

Our hope is that as you read and reflect you will find yourself in the pages. You will be able to apply the thoughts, examples, and prayers to your own life. Ultimately, after going through this book, we pray you will experience His peace surrounding you. True, lasting peace is found in the presence of Jesus. May you find His loving embrace and encouraging voice within these pages.

Many Blessings,

Elise, Jodi, Michele, and Jess

# His Peace Is Stronger Than Our Fears

By Jodi Kinasewitz

But now, this is what the Lord says—he who created you, Jacob, he who formed you, Israel: "Do not fear, for I have redeemed you; I have summoned you by name;

## you are mine.

When you pass through the waters, I will be with you; and when you pass through the rivers, they will not sweep over you. When you walk through the fire, you will not be burned; the flames will not set you ablaze.

**Isaiah 43:1-2 NIV**

# His Peace Is Stronger Than Our Fears

Worry...the pit in our stomachs, the dryness of our mouths, sweaty palms, sleepless nights, the rapid racing of our hearts. Our minds imagining the worst that could possibly happen. We've all experienced this, and it's not pleasant. We worry about our jobs, the health of our children, and the happiness of our spouses. We get caught up in the stressors of everyday life: What will we wear? What will we eat? Where should we go on vacation? Will the weather be nice for our outdoor party? The endless loop of questions – how? when? why? what if? – can take us on a treacherous ride that will harm our bodies, minds, and spirit. If we don't surrender to the fact that this is God's world and He is in control, we will live in a constant state of tension, robbing us of the joy and peace that He readily offers. I know from firsthand experience "letting go and letting God" is more difficult than it sounds.

A few years ago, I suffered through a relentless season of insomnia. I was completely unable to find rest. The absence of rest elicited great anxiety, which in turn drove me down into depths of depression. My days began with me awakening with a jolt, before the alarm even went off, mostly because I wasn't experiencing a real, deep sleep anyway. My heart pounded out of my chest before my feet hit the floor. I stumbled through the emotions of washing my face, brushing my teeth, and pulling on my workout clothes. I cried my way through my mornings. Tears fell while I was in desperate pleas of prayer with God, as I drank my first cup of coffee, as I plodded through my workouts hoping to maintain some semblance of health. More tears fell as I got dressed and drove myself to work.

Tears fell out of desperation, out of frustration, and out of fear. I was living scared. I muddled my way through my workday, drove home in dread of facing another evening riddled with anxiety and sadness rather than the joy of spending time with my loving husband and our four amazing kids. I survived the evening, a shell of myself, always preoccupied with thoughts of worry over the anticipation of yet another sleepless night. I went on "living" like this for almost six months. I kept pushing through and continued stuffing my feelings down.

I tried so hard to "give it to God." I begged Him to take it away. I pleaded with Him multiple times a day. I asked Him all the questions:
"Why is this happening to me?"
"How much longer, Lord?"
"Are you preparing me for something much more difficult?"

I was praying to God, I was laying my requests before Him, but I wasn't completely trusting Him. Instead of surrendering my concerns to Him and having full confidence He would take care of me, I continued to speak of my worries and fears. I wasn't thanking Him for the answers I trusted would come. Therefore, I remained in a state of tension and despair.

After several months of doctor and counseling appointments, trial and error with a variety of medications, and time off from my teaching job, the answers started to appear. God was using this time, this struggle, to renew me. He carried me through the fiery furnace to show me His strength. I had become quite complacent in my faith and self-sufficient in my everyday living. This season of despair taught me that I, in and of myself, am not enough.

However, I am more than enough when I live in step with God. He was restoring and renewing me, by showing me when I face life's toughest battles with Him at my side and have His Word as my armor, I will claim victory. He was breaking me open so his light could shine more radiantly in and through me.

Friends, if we aren't careful, these "little," "everyday" worries will slowly stack themselves, one on top of the other. The weight from the tower of worry will become more than we can bear. Our unhealthy fears will lead to doubt and shame. While these concerns about our future, our relationships, the health of our loved ones, and our financial stability are realistic concerns, God has commanded us to trust Him and relinquish control into His hands.

He tells us, *"But now, this is what the Lord says—he who created you, Jacob, he who formed you, Israel: "Do not fear, for I have redeemed you; I have summoned you by name; you are mine. When you pass through the waters, I will be with you; and when you pass through the rivers, they will not sweep over you. When you walk through the fire, you will not be burned; the flames will not set you ablaze."* (Isaiah 43:1-2 NIV).

God knows full well the worries that weigh us down. He does not want us to live this life alone, apart from Him. Instead, God asks us to pour out our hearts to Him - trusting He is actively working for our good. God created us. He ordained every moment of our lives. He loves us. He made it very clear we would have troubles in this world, but He has also promised to go before us and with us. When we finally release control and give it to God, when we acknowledge and accept our battles for what they are, and when we start putting all of our faith and confidence in the Lord, we will be set free.

Let's open our minds and soften our hearts to the idea that God is using it all for good. Whether it be waves of anxiety, slow-burning fires of depression, or another adversity, we must hold on to the hope that God is building our perseverance and endurance. He is restoring and refining our faith. When we surrender our hearts and minds to the King of all Kings, we will see His peace is much stronger than our fears.

## Reflection Questions

What are some of the worries you carry on a daily basis? How does the weight of these worries wear your spirit down? How is God inviting you to lay your worries down, and how can you surrender your worries to Him?

_____

_____

_____

_____

_____

_____

_____

_____

_____

_____

_____

_____

_____

_____

_____

_____

_____

_____

_____

## Prayer

Heavenly Father, thank you that you promise to give the weak,
weary, worried, hurried, and distracted peace and comfort.
Thank you for your compassion, love, and eternal grace. May
you guide us to opportunities to be a fountain of love and
grace for ourselves and others. May we seek to be with you
and build your kingdom rather than accomplish everything on
our to-do lists. Ease our worries, Lord, and help us to rest in
your arms of peace knowing you go before us and beside us in
all things. Amen.

# Trading My Panic-Stricken Thoughts

By Elise Daly Parker

"You will keep him in

# perfect peace

Whose mind is stayed on You,
Because he trusts in You."

**Isaiah 26:3 NKJV**

# Trading My Panic-Stricken Thoughts

I sat in the chair, nearly twitching with anxiety. I was having a blue light treatment to get rid of several precancerous spots on my face.

I have fair, Irish skin and way too much sun damage. Like so many of us, I missed some of my regularly scheduled doctors' appointments during the early days of COVID. For years now, every time I go to the dermatologist, there are precancerous spots to treat. So, not surprisingly, by the time I got to my dermatologist, there were several precancerous lesions on my face and leg and even a patch of basal cell cancer on my arm. My doctor sprayed liquid nitrogen on the larger spots.

The blue light was a follow-up treatment to remove as many suspicious "lesions" as possible at once. The procedure is done with an application of acetone all over your face. Imagine intentionally inhaling large amounts of nail polish remover. Not pleasant! A topical drug is applied to prep the skin for the blue light. An hour later, the light treatment begins. I've had this done before to avoid several individual applications of stinging liquid nitrogen on obvious precancer spots that then blister. The blue light covers all the bases by treating the whole face. It feels a little like Pop Rocks as it targets the precancerous spots. There is some moderate stinging, burning, and redness for a couple of days after.

Nicole, the nurse, ushered me into the treatment room. She explained, "Put these goggles on. Then, I'm going to pull the blue light machine toward your face. I'll set the timer for 15 minutes and 40 seconds. Are you ready?"

*Wait a minute...I thought it was 13 minutes!* "I guess so. I'm feeling pretty anxious. I've got my music, though. I think I'll be okay," but I wasn't convinced.

"You'll be fine." Nicole pulled the machine in close, about three inches from my face. The machine surrounded the front and both sides of my head. The back of my head was against the examination chair. There wasn't much of an opening, except at the top of my head and below my chin. I didn't feel fine at all. I was completely gripped by anxiety. One hand clenched the chair, the other my iPhone. My earphones were already in my ears. I could feel my heart beating faster.

"Okay...ready?"
"Yes..."

Nicole stepped back from the machine. "Well, uh no," I cried as I pushed the machine away from my face. Nicole quickly stepped in so I didn't do any damage to myself or the machine. "I'm really not sure I can do this," I uttered. She said she'd give me a moment. My shoulders dropped as I took in a few deep breaths. "Dear Jesus, help me!" I settled a little deeper into the chair. *You can do this...*

Nicole stood waiting. "I know," she said, "It's hard, but you can do it."

"Okay, sorry...yes, I can do this. I'm ready."

Nicole pushed the blue light back over my face. Fear again flooded my body. Honestly, the way my body responded, it could've been a bad guy's hand with a rag soaked in chloroform coming toward me.

"Help me, dear Jesus."

The nurse left the room assuring me she'd check in.

The machine was loud. I had to turn up Lauren Daigle's *Look Up Child* album to drown out the menacing sounds. I couldn't open my eyes...I didn't want to be blinded by the light. So I fumbled until I found the volume control and cranked it up.

I calculated that after four or five songs, I'd be done. I knew God's Word and Truth is sprinkled throughout Lauren's lyrics. They became my prayer. If I drifted off Lauren's words, I was immediately in trouble. My mind went to scary thoughts like, "What if this machine malfunctions and blows up or something." I pictured the machine close to my face (not a good idea!) and that thought led to imagining myself confined to a very small dark room, like a prison, but darker and smaller. I also pictured myself pushing the machine away and running for the door. Yes, I was panicky and claustrophobic.

"You will keep in perfect peace whose mind is set on you...Please help me, Lord."

Returning to the music, I focused on every word, every line. They spoke of God's power, faith, being still...they soothed my anxious thoughts.

The words in Lauren Daigle's songs were like neon sign reminders that I am safe with Christ right there in the medical chair. No matter what, the Lord is with me, protecting me, sheltering me. I sensed His presence and felt secure.

I knew time was passing. When I strayed, I prayed. A few Scriptures came to mind. I botched some, but still they gave me comfort. I knew a friend was praying Philippians 4:6-8 over me – that I would not be anxious about anything – and that thought brought peace.

Suddenly, the whirring noises stopped and the light dimmed. I made it through. Relief and gratitude overcame me. I was done. By setting my mind on worship, prayer, and His Word, God had gotten me through. He gave me His peace when I couldn't muster up my own.

That's our God. He promises His peace if we stay focused on Him, if we trust Him. He delivers.

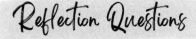

*Reflection Questions*

What do you do when you face a stressful circumstance? It may be a situation others could manage well, but for you it breeds anxiety. How has God shown up for you personally at a time when you needed peace? How do you "stay" your mind on Him?

_____

_____

_____

_____

_____

_____

_____

_____

## Prayer

Lord, you tell us that when we keep our minds focused on you
- when we trust you despite our circumstances - we will have
perfect peace. Thank you for the way you demonstrate this in
our lives. Thank you for allowing us to exchange our fear for
your peace. Help us, Lord, to remember to turn our minds
over to you when anxiety threatens to take over.
In Jesus' name I pray, Amen.

# You Are Not Alone

## By Michele Wilbert

When anxiety was
great within me,
your consolation
brought me

Psalm 94:19 NIV

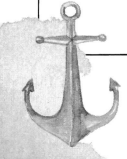

# You Are Not Alone

Anxious thoughts can masquerade in perfectly curated IG feeds, a well-written blog on how to live a balanced life, and in picture-perfect family photos.

They hide in messy buns and comfy clothes. They get in step with your choreography for your latest TikTok and seat themselves next to you in the boardroom.

They play hide-and-seek at your child's playdates and they interrupt your conversations with friends.

These thoughts even find invitations to your celebrations of achievement. They would lead you to believe you are all alone, but you are not.

Gallup Research reports in a worldwide survey "nearly four in 10 adults say their lives have been affected to some degree by depression and anxiety."[1] 42% of Americans experience anxiety and depression. The world's most famous poets, presidents, and even preachers have battled their anxious thoughts.

In fact, we read a real account about a hero of the faith and a prophet of God in I Kings 18 who, at the pinnacle of success in ministry, experienced great depression.

Elijah directed Ahab to summon the people from all over Israel. Elijah stood before them and spoke out against their double-mindedness in worshiping both Baal and Yahweh.

1 "Serious Depression, Anxiety Affect Nearly 4 in 10 Worldwide." Gallup Blog, October 20, 2021, https://news.gallup.com/opinion/gallup/356261/serious-depression-anxiety-affect-nearly-worldwide.aspx, accessed February 22, 2021.

He puts before the 450 prophets of Baal a contest to see whose God is real. Elijah proposes they each set up an altar and the God who answers with fire is the real God.

Nothing happens when the prophets of Baal dance around and call out to Baal. However, the Lord answers Elijah. Fire comes down and prophets are executed. God then sends rain and the drought is relieved.

As I Kings 18 details Elijah's ministry victory, I Kings 19 gives an honest account of Elijah's depression. After Elijah's triumphant win, Ahab's wife Jezebel threatens to take Elijah's life. He does not respond in retaliation or boast of his success. He fears for his life and asks the Lord to take his. Elijah runs and hides under a broom tree.

Have you had that happen? One text message in the middle of a great day or a comment from your boss or friend in a brief conversation that sends your thoughts spiraling and you running?

James 5:17 reminds us Elijah was human just like us. We can all relate to Elijah. Anxiety and depression can come upon people during good times. Exhaustion, worry, and uncertainty can make us want to give up or run and hide.

God was still walking with Elijah. His story can shape how we respond to our anxious thoughts:

- **REST (I Kings 19:3-9)**

Elijah had enough. He was ready to give up. God let Elijah sleep, eat, refuel, and rest. God met his physical needs.

- **REASSURANCE (I Kings 19:9-13)**

After a time of rejuvenation, God sent Elijah on a 40-day journey and revealed himself in a gentle whisper. God reminded Elijah He was with him. Elijah was not alone.

- **RE-ENGAGE (I Kings 19:13-18)**

Elijah's anxious thoughts didn't disqualify him from serving God. God asked Elijah, "What are you doing here?" God's response is not what you would expect. God still had work for Elijah to do.

## Reflection Questions

How can you respond to God working in your life in this season? What thoughts do you need to fight today with God's truth? Have you wrestled with anxious thoughts, believing you are the only one? Do you need rest, reassurance, or to re-engage? Are you letting something in life masquerade as peaceful living?

_____

_____

_____

_____

_____

_____

_____

_____

_____

_____

_____

## Prayer

Heavenly Father, thank you that you know our anxious
thoughts and meet us in the middle of them. Thank you for
providing everything we need and your reassurance that you
are with us. Help us chase down our anxious thoughts and
exchange them for the truths of Scripture and give us your
peace. Give us the courage today to obey by the power of your
Spirit. In your name, Jesus, Amen.

# Peace Like a River

## By Jess Carey

For this is what the Lord says:
"Behold, I extend

# peace to her

like a river,
And the glory of the nations like
an overflowing stream;
And you will be nursed, you will
be carried on the hip and rocked
back and forth on the knees.
As one whom his mother
comforts, so I will comfort you;
And you will be comforted in
Jerusalem."

**Isaiah 66:12-13 NASB**

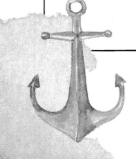

34

# Peace Like a River

I grew up near the Mississippi River, which is wide, muddy, and powerful. Watching the river offers a consistent view. The only way to know the water you are now seeing isn't the water you just saw is the occasional barge, boat, or debris caught up in the movement. I remember how the "Mighty Mississippi," would carry giant trees like toothpicks during flood stage.

I was taught as a young girl to respect the river. We were not allowed to wade out into the water, not even a few feet. The Mississippi, unlike other more gentle rivers, has strong undercurrents and whirlpools. They will pull anything under and downstream in a matter of seconds. So a river isn't the image I would normally associate with the passage above. Shouldn't peace be more like a gently flowing brook? What if peace looks a little different than we suspect?

This passage from Isaiah is a prophetic nod to the Messiah bringing peace to Jerusalem. The idea is that God would send the Messiah to bring safety and completeness to the Jews. It's not just for Jews though, the second part of verse 12 mentions the "glory of the nations," which translated means the Gentiles. So the Messiah is going to bring safety and completeness to the Jews and the Gentiles. No small feat. The Messiah would bring peace like a river that flows continuously and never ends. He would ultimately do it through a violent end.

When Jesus entered Jerusalem just before He was crucified, He came in peace. He rode into the city, on a donkey, waving to a crowd, who would soon turn on him (Matthew 21:1-11).

The picture of Jesus weeping for the city that would soon condemn Him to the cruelest death is humbling. He knew what He was going to face. Rather than being filled with overwhelming anxiety and fear, He is filled with peace and compassion.

This image is what reminded me of the "Mighty Mississippi." On the surface, Jesus strolled through the streets, preached publicly in the synagogues, and healed the people. He "flowed downstream" as was His usual custom, but the WILD undercurrent that threatened Him was present the entire time. The threat and doom of the crucifixion were churning beneath the surface.

The whirlpools and undercurrents are part of the river, but they don't bother the river. The river is not anxious about its backward flow. The river keeps moving forward in a steady stream. When the undercurrents pull debris down and toss it back and forth, the chaos of that moment doesn't stop the flow. The river consumes the chaos and carries everything forward because that is its purpose. Jesus didn't allow the plotting of the Pharisees or the fickle crowd to steal His peace.

So what did Jesus do to have peace like a river?

- He continued to pray - "Jesus went out as usual to the Mount of Olives, and his disciples followed him." Luke 22:39 NIV
- He did his regular job of teaching and preaching - "Jesus entered the temple courts, and, while he was teaching, the chief priests and the elders of the people came to him..." Matthew 21:23 NIV
- He didn't defend himself - "Meanwhile Jesus stood before the governor, and the governor asked him, 'Are you the king of the Jews?' 'You have said so,' Jesus replied." Matthew 27:11 NIV

When we face circumstances that threaten our peace, we can adopt the pattern of Jesus. We pray so we will have the stamina to endure our trials and tribulations. We continue to do the work God has called us to do in our day-to-day. Lastly, we don't worry and endlessly rehearse our defense. We speak the truth and allow God to defend us.

## Reflection Questions

What areas of your life feel like a whirlpool of chaos? How can you submit those to the river of peace that Jesus offers? How would you describe a river of peace? Babbling brook or Mighty Mississippi? How is Jesus like both?

_____

_____

_____

_____

_____

_____

_____

_____

_____

_____

_____

_____

_____

_____

_____

_____

_____

_____

_____

## Prayer

Dear Jesus, you are my source and example of peace. I desire to have peace like a river. I want to be complete and safe. You demonstrated what it means to have peace everlasting in dire circumstances. Please help me stay grounded in the power of your peace. Flow through me as I pray, work, and surrender myself to your will. Amen.

# Letting Go, Knowing God Is Holding On

By Jodi Kinasewitz

"For I know the plans I have for you," declares the Lord, "plans to prosper you and not to harm you, plans to give you

# hope

and a future."

**Jeremiah 29:11 NIV**

# Letting Go, Knowing God Is Holding On

It was her first day of kindergarten. Anna, adorned with her adorable back-to-school hairdo, colorful gingham dress, and purple backpack, flashed her excited, "Here I come, World!" smile as she clumsily climbed the stairs onto the big yellow bus. She glanced back for one more wave, her ocean blue eyes filled with anticipation locking in on mine brimming with tears.

It can't be true that my vivid memories, etched ever so clearly in my mind, were more than a decade ago. But it is true. And now here I am, on the brink of launching my baby out into the world.

In the midst of all the hustle, in a quiet moment with God, it dawned on me that I was experiencing the same worries I had on my daughter's first day of kindergarten. My mind and heart were harboring endless concerns: *Is she scared? Will she meet new friends easily? What happens if she gets sick and I'm not there to care for her? Who will hug her when she is sad? Catch her tears when she is lonely? Remind her to get enough sleep?*

I was blathering in an attempt to pray the perfect prayer over Anna and myself during this roller-coaster ride of emotions. I was flailing - the words would not come, but the tears streamed down my cheeks. And then, with one big inhale and exhale, a sense of calm washed over me. I felt the presence and peace of the Holy Spirit reminding me that God is in control. I was released from the self-induced burden of praying the perfect prayer and comforted in the reminder that He is the creator and author of Anna's story and mine. He has blessed us this far in life, so I needn't worry that He'd fail us now.

Parenting is one of God's greatest blessings, but it can also elicit our worry and need for prayer the most. Our kids are within the loving borders of our nests for only so long. Then they are off, flying on their own, as God intended. As parents, we can learn to let go, knowing He is holding on to all of us. We can hold onto God's promise of perfect peace as we learn to let go, as we watch our kids grow up and move out. This next step is not about God blessing our plans for our kids' lives. But rather, it is about us relinquishing control and worry so we can bear witness to the beautiful story He is sure to tell in and through them.

How do we let go and hand over control? How do we assure our kids that everything is going to be okay? How do we remind ourselves that His plans are perfect and will lead to a peace-filled life?

We draw on our faith, we turn to God's Word, and we remind ourselves and our kids of His promise, "Be strong and courageous. Do not be frightened, and do not be dismayed, for the Lord your God is with you wherever you go" (Joshua 1:9). We help our children view this new chapter of their lives through the lens of God's sovereignty.

Our faithful following of Jesus is the best example we can set for our children. Being obedient to God's calling on our lives as their parents, leading them in His way, reminding them they are to do His will - this is how we can lead them to the path of His peace. We can ask God to give us the wisdom we need to release our grip on our children's lives. God gifted them to us. Let's give our children back to Him, trusting He will do His good works in and through them.

Remember all the times we wished away the sleepless nights, nap schedules, potty training, shoe tying, swimming, and bike-riding lessons? Remember how endless they seemed? And now, we live the reality of how quickly they passed.

Remember the excitement over all their firsts? First word, first step, first day of kindergarten, first lost tooth, first sleepover, first time backing out of the driveway on their own. Those firsts came and went, but we'll cherish them forever. So let's get excited and let our hearts be filled with joy and peace thinking of all the glorious firsts God has in store for them in the next chapters of their lives. "'For I know the plans I have for you,' declares the Lord, 'plans to prosper you and not to harm you, plans to give you hope and a future'" (Jeremiah 29:11).

Saying goodbye, or moving on from one phase of our kids' lives to another – whether it's transitioning from baby to toddler, toddler to school age, or teenage to moving out of the house – may seem unbearable. Yet, we can hold tight to all the memories and walk in the peace of His presence. We can trust in God's promise and plans for our future and the futures of our children.

## Reflection Questions

What worries about your children are weighing heavy on your heart? How can you rest in God's presence and peace as you learn to "let go"?

_____

_____

_____

_____

_____

_____

_____

_____

_____

_____

## Prayer

Oh Lord, relieve us of the overwhelming grief and worry we are feeling right now, and replace it with hope and excitement for our child's new phase of life. Release us from worrying about things beyond our control, and remind us that despite the inevitable challenges our children face as they grow up, you're directing their path. Release us from feeling like our time as "mom" is over and help us find meaningful ways to stay connected and deepen our relationships with our kids in this new season. Lord, hold us tightly in your peace and comfort as we release our kids to you, knowing you have the perfect story written for their lives. Amen.

# A Sunrise Encounter

## By Elise Daly Parker

"Come to me, all you who are weary and burdened, and I will give you rest.
Take my yoke upon you and learn from me, for I am gentle and humble in heart,
and you will

# find rest

for your souls.
For my yoke is easy and my burden is light."

**Matthew 11:28-30 NIV**

# A Sunrise Encounter

Overcome with worry, fear, and, truth be told, a lack of faith, I cried out to God, "Where are you? I need you to send me a sign that you're with me."

It had been a particularly difficult time. My relationships with a couple of family members were strained. We didn't see eye-to-eye on some issues. I was concerned, enough to be tossing and turning at night. I woke up many mornings for a few weeks at 4 am with my thoughts racing, my heart pounding. I couldn't get back to sleep...until around 6 am. Then, I would start to dose off right when it was time to "wake up" so I could get to my exercise class.

My rhythm was all off. I was tempted every morning to hit the snooze button. But I knew that would only make matters worse. Exercise gave me a daily jolt of energy and got those endorphins going, even in my harried state. I also squeezed in a few minutes of God-time before I left for the gym. Though it was feeling forced, that too I knew was helping a little as I fought the battle of despair and hopelessness.

I pulled on my workout clothes, brushed my teeth, and headed downstairs to my favorite chair perched by my bay window. The sun was rising bright and orange right above the tree-line. Time to head out.

The cold threatened to send me back to the warm embrace of my home, but no, I'd push forward. I didn't want to miss the exercise warmup – that was the best part. I turned on the car and blasted the defrost while I scraped ice off my windows. I was starting to run a little late...

The streets were still mostly dark, but the sun was continuing to rise. Its glow shone through the back of my car windows as I hurried toward my class. When I was just about there, I turned my head right and left before moving through the intersection. The golden hue caught my eye. I heard God beckoning, *Turn left*.

*But that's away from my class!*

I knew better than to argue. When God speaks, you listen. After I turned the corner, I was overcome by the most brilliant sky I've ever seen. Deep red, fuchsia, gold, coral, purple bands like strata lit the sky as the fiery orb rose over New York City. I continued down the street until I reached the STOP sign. Again, I heard that still small voice. *Stop! Slow down...this is for you today. Take it in!*

I sat there for a couple of minutes and took in the breathtaking view. I was in such a rush – demanding God give me a sign that He was near, assuring me He saw me in my agony – I nearly missed what He had waiting for me. I smiled as a sense of calm and well-being fell over me like a warm hug.

I was okay. I could trust God with all my worries and cares. He promises to make our burdens light, but we have to hand them over. I was ready to relinquish my anxiety in exchange for His peace. I asked God for a sign, and He delivered in living-color glory.

I've had a sleepless night or two in the years since that encounter. But when I start to fret, I am reminded of that sunrise and how God met me in my pain. I hand over my struggles again...and He is always there, ready to lift the weight of my burdens and restore rest even in the midst of my weariness.

# Reflection Questions

Sometimes, God speaks to me in a song, conversation, a series of God-incidences, and, in this case, the sunrise. How about you? Can you recall a time when God was communicating with you? How did He meet you when you were carrying a heavy burden? How did He lighten your load and give you rest? What heavy load are you carrying now that needs to be lightened?

_____

_____

_____

_____

_____

_____

_____

_____

_____

_____

_____

_____

_____

_____

_____

_____

_____

_____

_____

_____

_____

_____

_____

_____

## Prayer

Lord, thank you for your invitation to come to you! What a
gift to be able to draw near to you, to share our burdens that
feel too heavy to carry. Thank you for the way you assure us
and bring us rest through your Word, a song, a sunrise. Help
us slow down, listen, and not miss your still small voice in the
midst of our anxious thoughts. Allow us, Lord, to trust you
with our heavy loads. We pray in Jesus' name, amen.

# God's Peace in Rough Waters

## By Michele Wilbert

The Lord is my shepherd;
I have what I need.
He lets me lie down in green pastures; he
leads me beside quiet waters.

# He renews my life;

he leads me along the right paths
for his name's sake.
Even when I go through the darkest
valley, I fear no danger,
for you are with me, your rod and your
staff—they comfort me. You prepare a
table before me in the presence of my
enemies; you anoint my head with oil;
my cup overflows.
Only goodness and faithful love will
pursue me all the days of my life,
and I will dwell in the house of the Lord
as long as I live."

**Psalm 23:1-6 CSB**

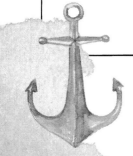

58

# God's Peace in Rough Waters

Late spring on the Ocoee River in Tennessee, the water flows fast and, as the river narrows, rafts experience larger rapids. The guide took us through the paces and the importance of listening to his commands, "Paddle forward, paddle, paddle!" "Now, paddle back, paddle, paddle!" and another important command, "Lean in!"

Getting us stuck in the eddies, he demonstrated the power of water and how to navigate the current. Trained river raft guides can show you how to use the river to slow down or speed up so you can turn your raft in the direction you want to go.

In preparation to enter what is known as Humongous – an area with large waves squeezed between large boulders followed by a large hole – the guide kept us wedged between rocks, watching the rafts farther ahead of us.

A person can quite literally find themselves up a river without a paddle or overboard without the experience of a guide.

Fear gripped us as we watched an entire raft overturn and paddles fly. We watched the life jackets surface and people gasping for air. As one by one the rafters got back in the raft, there was still one rafter missing.

Farther beyond the white caps, we saw a bright yellow jacket bobbing and even farther than that, we watched rescue workers scurry to throw a large black net across the river to help retrieve the rafter. Our guide went back over the safety basics of what to do when you go over, "Pull up your feet and point them downstream if you can't grab the boat."

At this point, you could hear the collective heart palpitations of everyone on the raft.

"Ready? Paddle!" he instructed. As we made our way through the narrow section between the rocks, he yelled, "Lean in!" Our raft hit the rapids with such force, the front of the boat launched out of the water and the back took on water. Out of the raft the front paddler went. Without hesitation, the guide continued to give instructions to the rest of us steering us through this rough section as he pulled our friend back in the boat. Before we knew it, we had made our way to calm, still waters at the end of the river.

As we read the words of Psalm 23, the psalmist describes a good shepherd who comes alongside us protecting us with every strength. Verse 5 affirms care in emergencies and it is overflowing with provision. Lastly, verse 6 closes with a reminder that goodness and love will pursue us all the days of life.

## Reflection Questions

> What is your response when life's circumstances toss you out of the boat and you are swept up by rapids and drowning? Have you found yourself stuck in places, unsure how to navigate rough waters? What voices are you listening to when faced with adversity, the world's or the Good Shepherd's?

_____

_____

_____

_____

_____

_____

_____

_____

_____

_____

_____

_____

_____

## Prayer

Father, help us to listen to your voice when we face life's difficulties. When we are pulled out of the boat and into rough water, give us strength to rely on you to lead us to still waters and give us your peace. Thank you for being our Helper, our Comforter and the one who renews our life. You are everything we need. In Jesus' name, Amen.

# Disarming Discontent

## By Jess Carey

Finally, brothers, rejoice.
Aim for restoration,
comfort one another,
agree with one another,

# live in peace;

and the God of love and peace
will be with you.

**2 Corinthians 13:11 ESV**

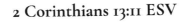

64

# Disarming Discontent

Recently, I noticed the utter lack of help I was receiving with chores around my house. I work full-time, volunteer at church, try to raise two decent humans, and stay happily married. I came home from a long day at work to find all the breakfast dishes still swimming in the dirty sink water, a pile of clean clothes unfolded in their basket, and a trail of shoes kicked off haphazardly throughout the house. I was ready to relax and all I felt was irritation.

Instead of calmly asking my entire family to help me tidy up things, I began slinging shoes into baskets, whipping clothes out of the laundry like a matador taming a bull, and throwing dishes into the dishwasher with enough force I'm surprised they didn't break. Suddenly, the minions I live with went on high alert. They crept out of their respective hiding places and began gingerly helping me.

I was already on the rampage. I was well past the moment that they COULD have helped without repercussions. It was at this moment my husband made the gravest mistake of all.

"What's the matter honey?" he asked.

The fireworks that went off in my head made me dizzy. I gathered what patience I had left in me to respond through gritted teeth. I knew better than to lie and say I was fine.

"I just finished a full day at work to come home to a house where no one seems to be willing to pick up after themselves. If I don't leave a list, yell, and start slamming things around no one is willing to help out," I retorted.

Then he responded with the most logical response.

"Did you ask for help?"

It was at this moment I had a choice. I could go nuclear, or I could recognize that he was right, settle my rage, and ask for help.

"Finally, brothers, rejoice. Aim for restoration, comfort one another, agree with one another, live in peace; and the God of love and peace will be with you." 2 Corinthians 13:11 ESV

Live in peace were the words that began to bubble up into my heart. I turned to my kids and my husband and broke down almost in tears.

"You guys, I cannot do everything on my own anymore. Mom used to be at home most of the day and I could manage all the dishes, laundry, cooking, and tidying. I have been working all day and I'm tired. I have tried for the past week to continue to patiently do everything and I don't sit down until I go to bed just so I can do it all over again the next day. You guys, I'm exhausted," I confessed.

Then the last half of the verse above came to fruition. The God of love and peace was with me.

"Mommy, I'm sorry I haven't been helpful. What can I do?" my son asked. Then my daughter chimed in. "Yeah, Mom, I can help. I can make dinner sometimes," she offered.

"Thank you, kids. We all need to help Mom." My husband agreed. Then we went on to have a discussion about how each member of the family could help alleviate the burden I was feeling.

It hasn't been perfect since that moment and I know I will need to do lots of reminding, but I was so grateful I didn't allow the seed of bitterness to blossom toward my family. I was reminded that sometimes living in peace requires us to seek reconciliation. Living in peace requires us to forgive, extend grace, and speak up when we have a need. Sometimes being a peacekeeper looks like being someone willing to engage in conflict resolution. Hard to do, but well worth the peace that restoration provides.

How can we live in peace with one another?

1. Pause - reflect before you react.
2. Express our feelings and desires calmly.
3. Give grace when people forget or fail.
4. Work as a team to resolve disagreements.
5. Do not harbor resentment or hold grudges.
6. Forgive and move on.

## Reflection Questions

Is there someone you need to pursue restoration or peace with? How would your situation change if you were able to freely express yourself calmly? What would restoration with them look like? What do you stand to lose if you don't reconcile?

_____

_____

_____

_____

_____

## Prayer

Dear Jesus, sometimes we struggle to ask for what we need. Help us to be open and honest with others about our feelings and our needs. Lord, we desire to do this with a patient and loving heart so we can cultivate peace in our lives. Please reveal people we need to reconcile with and help us have the words to start the conversation. Jesus, you forgave, help us to forgive others so we can walk in your peace. Amen.

# Peace on Purpose

By Jodi Kinasewitz

"You will seek me and

# find me

when you seek me
with all your heart."

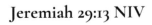

**Jeremiah 29:13 NIV**

# Peace on Purpose

It was a rainy, cold, Monday morning - nothing to be happy or excited about really. I parked in my usual spot at school and dashed into the building attempting to avoid all the puddles. As I walked into our teacher workroom, my rain jacket and umbrella dripping cold water all over the floor, I greeted my coworker with a smile and genuine, "Hey, how are you? Happy Monday! How was your weekend?"

She sluggishly turned from the Keurig where she was brewing her morning cup of coffee, and in a defeated demeanor asked, "How are you always so happy? Only you could come bouncing in here on a cold, rainy Monday all smiles and chatty."

While I was a bit caught off guard by her response, I didn't really think much of it. I put my lunch in the refrigerator, filled my Tervis with water, and headed to my room. As I was getting my teaching materials ready for the day, I thought more about what my coworker asked me – *how, or why, am I generally a very happy, joy-filled person? What do I have working in my favor that my coworker, or others I know, don't have? What do I experience that gives me this deep well of internal joy?* As I reflected on this more throughout my day, I realized my morning routine benefits me in so many ways. Along with exercise and giving myself enough time to ease into my day by not hitting the ground running, I have intentional quiet time with God. I pray, meditate, read my Bible, and journal every single morning.

The next day when I saw that same coworker, I told her I had an answer for why I feel joy, even on a cold, rainy, Monday morning, and where that joy comes from.

I went on to explain my morning routine and my intentional, scheduled time with God each day. After I shared with her that I spend time with God each morning, a hint of a smile crossed her face. As she turned to walk out of the break room she mumbled, "Maybe I should give that a try."

If you're anything like me, you are certain to schedule time for meals, exercise, social events, doctor appointments, learning opportunities, and Sabbath. In an effort to take care of our physical and mental health, we fuel our bodies with food, water, exercise, and overall self-care. But I wonder... *Are we intentionally scheduling time with God? Are we actively pursuing and seeking Him? Are we looking for Him, and to Him, as we move through our days?*

Friend, we have to come to the realization that just as we fuel our bodies and minds with life-giving resources, we have to fill our spiritual cups by seeking God on purpose. We are always safe and secure in His presence, but as we hustle through our busy days and become overwhelmed with our tasks and feelings, we often lose sight of His provision and promise. He has told us He will never leave us or forsake us. If we have a personal relationship with Jesus and have chosen to follow His way, nothing can prevent us from reaching Heaven. Even though this is our eternal promise, we can, and still do, lose sight of Him. We forget He is with us and this often leads to feelings of fear.

This is why we must be intentional about seeking God. If we want a life of peace, we must be diligent in pursuing Him purposefully. When we practice the daily discipline of walking and talking with Jesus as we would a dear friend, His peace will displace our fears.

You may be wondering what this looks like...How do we seek God on purpose?

Well, just as we schedule time for our workouts, meals, appointments, social activities, and rest, we must be adamant about blocking off time in our days to spend with just Him. No distractions, noise, no phone – just us and Him. This time can be spent in prayer, singing worship songs, reading the Bible, memorizing Scripture, journaling prayer requests and praises, or just sitting in complete silence in His presence. What really matters is we are completely present with Him. That's all He desires, us to seek Him with all of our hearts. Our intentional time with God is not an item to check off our to-do lists. In contrast, it is calling on God anytime, anywhere, all throughout our days. It can be as simple as a whisper, "Jesus, come near, I need you." He yearns for us to want Him above all else.

The world tells us if we want to be happy, we should fill our every desire – seek our physical, emotional, mental needs above all else. But for a true renewal of our minds and everlasting peace, we must practice a spiritual discipline of spending time with God in prayer and in reading our Bible. If we don't, it doesn't matter how physically fit we are or how many material items we possess, we will feel trapped, heavy, and burdened.

With our daily spiritual discipline in place - Will we still have bad moments in our days? Yes. Will we still have doubts and fears? Yes. But we will also have a peace that surpasses all understanding because we will be walking hand in hand with Jesus. We will find Him when we seek Him with all our hearts. We can breathe easy in His presence when we seek His peace on purpose.

# Reflection Questions

How will you take the time to be present with God?
When and where in your day will you plan to pursue
Him and His peace with purpose? What kind of peace
have you experienced in your life when you have
actively sought out Jesus? What are some fears you
currently have that need to be displaced with His peace?

_____

_____

_____

_____

_____

_____

_____

_____

_____

_____

_____

_____

_____

_____

_____

_____

_____

_____

_____

_____

_____

_____

## Prayer

Heavenly Father, thank you for being with us at all times. Even when we are tired, stressed, and full of worries, you give us peace that surpasses all understanding. Please intercede and plant in us a desire to seek you and your wisdom. Calm our racing minds and troubled hearts as you provide us new mercies each morning. Help us remember our prayers don't have to be fancy, but that calling out to you throughout our day is our best defense. We trust your love, God, and know that one day we will see you face to face. The joy we now experience by faith will be seen by sight. Amen.

# When Your No Leads To Peace

## By Elise Daly Parker

For you created my inmost being; you knit me together in my mother's womb.
I praise you because I am fearfully and

# wonderfully

made; your works are wonderful, I know that full well.

**Psalm 139:13-14 NIV**

# When Your No Leads To Peace

I was scurrying...running from activity to activity.

Because of my schedule, I felt nearly breathless and a little hysterical much of the time. I brushed it off as "just a busy season," knowing I couldn't keep up this pace. But what else could I do? I had to keep going, right?

My kids needed me.
My husband needed me.
My church needed me.
My ministry needed me.
My kids' teachers needed me.
My friends needed me.

I needed me to put my head down, plow through, and just keep going...

But I was spread so thin I didn't really feel present no matter where I was.

When I was with my kids, I was thinking about the phone calls I had to make for the ministry I was leading. Time with my husband? Well, he was a patient man. He could wait. When I showed up at my book group, I was embarrassed because, well, no, I hadn't actually read the book. And when I went to a party on a Saturday evening, it was fun for a bit. But then I had to dash to the next activity that happened to be the same night.

I couldn't say no...could I? I mean this was all good stuff.

I was showing up where I was needed, fulfilling my commitments. I was trying to be a good friend by saying yes...even though I had already said yes to another engagement. I was trying to be there for my kids and husband. And I was trying to have some fun too. I got to my counselor's office – 15 minutes late, of course – and told my tale,

"I'm too busy. I'm doing so much. I'm frazzled most of the time. But I'm doing good things. What can I possibly not do? I just don't see a way out."

And she said, "Well, the good robs from the best." (She was loosely quoting Oswald Chambers, who said, "The good is always the enemy of the best.")

*Huh? What did that mean?*

As we continued our discussion, I understood. There are all these things we can do – and they all seem good to do. They *are* good to do! But, if you're out and about in your community and your energy and passion shows, people will ask for your help. And, if you're a people-pleaser and you'd like to feel valuable, worthy, and approved of, you'll likely say one (or two or three or more) too many yesses.

That's exactly where I was. I said way too many yesses, and they were robbing me of peace and joy. I was drained and depleted. It was time to learn to say no. I almost considered "no" a dirty word!

Was this easy? No! Why? Because I had an underlying as yet unidentified problem. I was desperate to feel valuable.

Deep down in the core of my being, I believed I had to earn love and approval by "doing." I didn't believe I was of value just because I existed...just because I was fearfully and wonderfully made by our good God, the creator Himself, though this is what He says. We are human beings...not human doings!

Old habits ingrained in unhealthy beliefs die hard. It took me a long time – many cycles of overcommitting. Then I'd have the aha moment, again. *Oh no, I've said yes to too much again.* And then I had to cut back yet again at the risk of disappointing others with my nos right in the midst of their needs.

I am so happy to report, now, when I am asked to do something new, commit to a project, invited somewhere, I am in the habit of saying, "I'll get back to you." I know I *must* consider this one thing in the context of all the other things. Quite often, I now even say, "No." I am in a much more peaceful place than ever before. And guess what? I am still loved!

## *Reflection Questions*

Do you say yes to too many commitments and end up feeling depleted? If you struggle with believing you are fearfully and wonderfully made, why do you think that is? What is at the root of saying yes to too much...and lacking peace? What is a no you need to consider?

_____

_____

_____

_____

_____

_____

_____

_____

_____

_____

## Prayer

Dear Lord, you love us so much, we can't even imagine it.
Your love is perfect and complete because you made us and
you take pleasure in your good works. Your love does not
depend on what we do or don't do. Will you please help us
accept your love? Will you help this one reading right now to
believe you truly love them because they are wonderfully
fearfully made? If they need to say no to something, will you
speak to them in their inmost being and give them clarity?
Order their steps and show them today you love them no
matter what they do or don't do. In Jesus' name, amen.

# What's Stealing Your Peace?

## By Michele Wilbert

And the

# peace of God,

which surpasses
all understanding,
will guard your hearts
and minds
in Christ Jesus.

**Philippians 4:7 CSB**

# What's Stealing Your Peace?

We placed two red ripe tomatoes, one large watermelon, and a bag of chips on the grocery store conveyor. We had all of our final ingredients for our first-day-of-summer picnic. As the cashier scanned the barcode and we heard the blip, it was music to our ears. The sound of summer beginning.

The cashier handed me the receipt, and said, "Have a great day!" My son shouted, "BEST SUMMER EVER! Right, Mom?"

We were ready to float all our cares away in the pool from the longest Covid, distance-learning, hybrid, back-to-school, part-time school year. All of a sudden, the fire alarm went off in the store, and we were startled out of our pool-floating dreams. The flashing lights and piercing sounds chirped so loud in the store I couldn't hear the cashier's instructions.

I looked around and everyone was holding their ears. The manager ran to the panel near the exit to shut it off, only she couldn't. I looked over and suddenly the watermelon my son held now had become an anchor and weighed him down.

I met his big blue eyes and looked straight in them and said, "You are okay. We are safe." I waited for the watermelon to drop and shatter. His fingers were tightly clenched around it, his body shaking, and he began to breathe faster with each second. The alarm didn't stop. I grabbed the tomatoes and chips and guided him out of the store. At last, inside the car, he desperately gasped for more air. As I loosened his fingers from his tight grasp on the watermelon, it only made the breathing worse and full panic set in. He needed something to hold onto to steady his breathing.

Have you been ready to celebrate the really good things in your life when all of a sudden something threatens to steal your peace? Christ's peace is contrary to anything this world offers. However, sometimes fear and lies can rob us of true peace. Oftentimes, the world will get us to believe our peace is at risk.

Philippians 4:7 teaches us that the peace of God surpasses our understanding. It is deeper and richer than anything we can comprehend. This verse assures us that the insurmountable peace of God guards our hearts and minds. Not only is the Lord's peace a prescription for our worries, fears, and troubled hearts, but it gives us hope that He is with us.

Right there in the back of the car, we asked God for His help. He answered. I slowly began to unpeel the now looser gripped fingers. My boy released the watermelon into my hands and exhaled. He smiled the peaceful smile of a child who knows they are safe.

## Reflection Questions

What is something stealing your peace currently? What steps can you take today to guard your heart and mind and remember Christ is with you? What is something you can hold onto to steady you? How can you ask God to help you let go of whatever it is that has a grip on you?

_____

_____

_____

_____

_____

_____

_____

_____

_____

_____

_____

_____

_____

## Prayer

Father, thank you that your peace is not of this world. Thank you that only you satisfy. I pray for the person today longing for peace in their current situation. Lord, you promise to guard our hearts and minds in Christ Jesus. Please bring peace that surpasses all understanding. In Jesus' mighty name. Amen.

# Peace –
# In Sickness
# and in Health

By Jess Carey

But He was pierced
for our transgressions,
He was crushed for our
iniquities;
the punishment that brought us
peace was on Him,
and by His wounds (stripes)
we are healed.

**Isaiah 53:5  NIV**

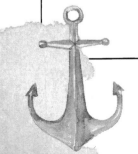

# Peace — In Sickness and in Health

"In sickness and in health," are the common wedding vows we have all heard. Most of us barely thought through this idea before we walked down the aisle. The exceptions are the rare couples who faced a health crisis before marriage. I don't think most couples consider what a life "in sickness" will be like. We eternally expect to be like we are at that moment, healthy. At least, that is what I thought when I walked down the aisle.

About three years ago, I woke up in the middle of the night with severe chest pains. I chalked it up to indigestion even though I had rarely struggled with that. The next morning, I called my sister who is a nurse to ask her opinion of the episode. She suggested I start a regimen of low-dose aspirin and call my doctor immediately. I followed her guidance. My doctor was unable to see me for over a week, so I waited patiently assuming if there was no "emergency" on their end I must be okay. Four days later, I was in the emergency room for another chest episode and a possible panic attack.

This set off a series of doctor visits with a cardiologist, pulmonary specialist, internist, and naturopath. None of them were able to diagnose why I was having irregular chest pains. I was deemed a medical mystery. I quickly learned why they call it "practicing medicine." No doctor had the answers. You can imagine my frustration in continuing to suffer without cause, relief, or any direction to find healing.

Trust me, I prayed, hoped, and believed for my healing. I read so many Scriptures on healing and continuously cried out in prayer for a touch from heaven. This mysterious illness carried on for over three years.

During this time I contracted COVID-19 and was bedridden for several days. It was during one of my feverish episodes with unbearable body aches I began speaking the verse from Isaiah over my body.

"But He was pierced for our transgressions, He was crushed for our iniquities; the punishment that brought us peace was on Him, and by His wounds (stripes) we are healed." Isaiah 53:5 NIV

"By His stripes, I am healed," I cried out in my bed. Tears streamed down my face as I writhed in pain. My husband came in to see how he could help. This triggered the whole family to come in and witness what was going on, including my daughter on FaceTime with my own mother. My mom, a nurse of over 40 years, soothed my aching body and spirit with her words.

"Jess, try to settle. Your body needs every ounce of energy right now. Take some painkillers and do your best to rest," she said.

I was an obedient daughter. I took my meds, curled myself into the most comfortable position I could find, and silently repeated, "By His stripes, I am healed." It must have been a few hours later that I woke up to intense heat in the left side of my ribcage (a common site for my chest pains). I knew Jesus was releasing healing in my body. I had read so many testimonies of people being healed and feeling heat run through the area of the body that was afflicted.

*I received my healing,* I thought. I knew I wasn't healed from COVID yet...but I believe the hot rush of healing power was released at that moment. As I write this, I haven't had a chest episode since.

Maybe you are experiencing a similar health concern. Maybe you are waiting on healing. From experience, a health crisis can steal our peace quickly. Panic replaces the promises of God when you are in pain. Just like marriage is a covenant, God is a covenant keeper. He keeps His promises. No matter whether you or someone you love is facing an "In sickness" season, I know the promise of God is that an "In health" season is on its way.

How do we have peace in a season of sickness?

1. Pray Scriptures like Isaiah 53:5 over the situation.
2. Seek wise counsel from your healthcare providers, but don't accept ANY diagnosis that doesn't align with the Word of God. Put up Scriptures of healing where you are reminded of those promises regularly.
   o Revelation 21:4
   o Mark 5:34
   o Psalm 147:3
   o 1 Peter 2:24
3. Ask the "elders" of your church to pray over you, anoint the sick, lay hands on you. James 5:14

# Reflection Questions

When you face sickness, what is your first emotion?
Does that emotion align with the Word of God? Do you
struggle to believe in the healing power of God for
yourself? For others? If so, how can you stir up your
faith in this area? If you are still waiting on healing, how
can you "wait in faith"?

_____

_____

_____

_____

_____

_____

_____

_____

_____

_____

_____

_____

_____

_____

_____

_____

_____

_____

_____

_____

_____

## Prayer

Dear Jesus, We desire to be people who trust your promises
for healing. Whether we are on the journey of healing or
standing beside a loved one, help us be full of faith. Jesus,
reveal to us testimonies of your healing power that will deepen
our beliefs in your willingness to heal. If there is anything in us
that prevents healing, please reveal it so we can repent and be
fully restored. In Jesus' name, amen.

Journal

# Journal

Journal

Journal

## Journal

_____

_____

_____

_____

_____

_____

_____

_____

_____

_____

_____

_____

_____

_____

_____

_____

_____

_____

_____

_____

_____

_____

_____

_____

# Jess Carey

Jess Carey is the award-winning author of *Chart a Course – Taking a Journey With God at the Helm.* Her writing has been featured in Christianparenting.org, focusonthefamily.com, and gritandvirtue.com. She is a wife of over 15 years and mother to two teenagers. From acting in New York to running an international business, she has had to overcome fear, insecurity, and perfectionism to pursue God's divine plan. She is passionate about helping every person do the same. Connect with Jess on Instagram @jess_careyaz, or her website www.jessicacarey.co

# Jodi Kinasewitz

Jodi lives in Mason, Ohio, with her husband of 20 years Matt, their four children, and their yellow lab, Max. She is an elementary-level reading specialist and a certified yoga instructor. She is passionate about leading Christian-inspired yoga classes, reading, and writing. She loves to travel with her family, and she spends any time she can outdoors. Jodi has had several articles published with various Christian platforms including gritandvirtue.com, mommentor.org, makemeavailable.com, and she was published in *Milk & Honey Women Devotional Journal, Volume 1*. Jodi's hope is by sharing her story of struggle through a season of anxiety and depression her writing will shine a light on the importance of mental health while pointing others to Jesus. Find out more about Jodi on Instagram @jkinasewitz, Facebook - Jodi Kinasewitz, and read more of her writing on her blog Living to Learn (jkinasewitz.wixsite.com/website).

# Elise Daly Parker

Elise Daly Parker is a certified life coach passionate about empowering moms to savor and not just survive this busy season of life with clarity, confidence, and calm. She does this through one-on-one and group coaching, workshops (Vision Boards are a fave!), and her podcast MomVision. Elise shares practical tips and openly shares her experiences – the good, the bad, the ugly – of being the mom of four now-grown daughters, 37 years of marriage, and continuing to become the woman she is meant to be. Elise is on a mission to help moms unapologetically – and with no shame or guilt – know, love, and accept themselves today, with the hope and promise of moving towards their goals and dreams for tomorrow. Find her at EliseDalyParker.com, on the MomVision podcast, @elisedalyparker on Instagram, and @elise.dalyparker on Facebook.

# Michele Wilbert

Michele is a writer, speaker, and entrepreneur who lives in California with her husband and son. An experienced marketing and public relations professional, she speaks to others about work as worship and finding your identity in Christ. She writes small group curriculum, devotions, and leadership development. She is a graduate of Dallas Theological Seminary and finds joy teaching others to study God's Word. Connect with her at www.michelelwilbert.com and on Instagram @michelelwilbert.

Made in the USA
Columbia, SC
15 April 2022

58849178R00063